♥ Rachael

God's blessings!

Alice Gray

July 2006

A gift for

Rachael ♡

♡

From

Grandma
With lots of love
tucked inside

It isn't the big pleasures
that count the most;
it's making a great deal
out of the little ones.

JEAN WEBSTER

KEEPSAKES
for a Mother's
HEART

Creating Cherished Moments for a Lifetime

ALICE GRAY & SUSAN WALES

COUNTRYMAN
®

Published in association with Loyal Arts Literary Agency, www.LoyalArts.com.

Project Manager—Lisa Stilwell
Cover photograph by Steve Gardner, PixelWorks Studios, ShootPW.com

ISBN 1-4041-0217-5

Thomas Nelson, Inc., P.O. Box 141000, Nashville, TN 37214
www.thomasnelson.com | www.jcountryman.com

Printed and bound in the United States of America

Contents

Preface

What the heart gives away is never gone...
It is kept in the hearts of others.

ROBIN ST. JOHN

The years of motherhood are filled with golden moments strung together by sunrises and sunsets. One moment we are singing lullabies to babes nestled in our arms—and in the next moment we are watching in wonder as our grown children step up to receive their diplomas. The years fly by so quickly. Where do all the keepsake moments go?

Because we live in such a hurry-up world, mothers are longing more than ever for the simple pleasures of home and family. It's as though we are searching for a rhythm to our lives that will offer more connectedness, more meaning, more treasured times. But too often, as mothers move through the busy seasons of life, these precious longings remain tucked away in a corner of our heart called *Someday*.

We understand the tender desires of a mother's heart, and that is why we have written this book—to help you find that golden pathway where simple pleasures can be richly celebrated and then kept in your heart as memories that bring joy for a lifetime.

So nestle into a cozy chair and dream with us about country walks, umbrella parades, teddy bear picnics, and bedtime prayers. Delight yourself with simple ideas that can turn ordinary days into magical ones. Allow your spirit to be sweetly refreshed by inspirational quotes and Scriptures. Linger over tender stories and let them sprinkle tranquility on your day.

As the pages unfold, you will discover a wonderful theme woven throughout this book. Very simply, even in life's hurried pace, you can treasure the golden moments of motherhood—not *someday*, but *every day*.

Alice and Susan

Mothers hold their children's hands
for a while…
their hearts, forever.

AUTHOR UNKNOWN

Golden Moments

Most of all the other beautiful things in life
come by twos and threes, by dozens and hundreds.
Plenty of roses, stars, sunsets, rainbows...
but only one mother in the whole world.

KATE DOUGLAS WIGGIN

Ordinary Days

Sometimes the moments of a child's life seem almost ordinary—
    ❦ Chasing butterflies
      ❦ Building sandcastles
        ❦ Blowing soap bubbles
          ❦ Discovering the wonder of a rainbow

Sometimes the moments of a mother's life seem almost ordinary, too—
    ❦ Rocking a child to sleep
      ❦ Kneeling at a bedside to pray
        ❦ Tucking love notes into lunchboxes
          ❦ Staying awake until a child comes home

But when all the tiny, incidental, everyday moments of a mother and child are woven together with love, they form the fabric of life—and those moments are no longer ordinary. They are golden.

TURNING ORDINARY DAYS INTO SPECIAL DAYS

Add a touch of delight to the most ordinary of days by creating simple pleasures. Here's a potpourri of ideas that will be as much fun for you as for your children.

- ❦ Using a permanent marker, write a love note on an inflated balloon. Deflate the balloon and tuck it inside your child's lunchbox, jacket pocket, or purse.

- ❦ Prop up a different special photo at each family member's place setting. During dinner, talk about the memory behind each photo.

- ❦ Treat your daughter to a candlelit bubble bath.

- ❦ Take your son out on a date to the restaurant of his choice and let him order dinner for you.

- ❦ Have a family Dress-Alike or Dress-in-the-Same-Color day.

❦ Celebrate a half-year birthday with half a cake and a simple gift.

❦ Once or twice a year, surprise your children by picking them up from school at lunchtime. Take them to a ball game, swing in the park, or ride a merry-go-round. Go bike riding, feed the birds, or just hold hands and take a leisurely walk on a country road.

❦ Put out a variety of candles, place mats, dishes, decorative napkins, and flowers. Let a child use these to creatively set the dinner table.

❦ Once in a while skip dinner and let everyone make a banana split.

❦ Plant bulbs in Grandma's garden that she won't find out about until spring when they bloom.

❦ At dusk, take a walk around your neighborhood and watch as windows unfold with light.

❦ Let your children decorate inexpensive white pillowcases with permanent markers or puffy paint. Afterward, invite the family for a slumber party in your bedroom.

❦ Walk barefoot in the summer rain—and leave the umbrellas at home!

❦ After you tuck the kids in bed, wait a couple of minutes and then flip on the lights and yell, "Pajama ride!" Wrap a blanket around them, scoot them into the car, then drive to the take-out window of a fast-food restaurant and order ice-cream cones. ❧

It isn't the big pleasures
that count the most;
it's making a great deal
out of the little ones.

JEAN WEBSTER

A Teddy Bear Picnic

If you go down in the woods today
You're sure of a big surprise.
If you go down in the woods today
You'd better go in disguise.
For ev'ry bear that ever there was
Will gather there for certain, because
Today's the day the teddy bears have their picnic.

FROM "THE TEDDY BEARS' PICNIC," LYRICS BY JIMMY KENNEDY

My husband Ken adores teddy bears so it is no surprise that when our granddaughter, Hailey, was born, "Bop" gave her a teddy bear almost twice her size. Teddy immediately became Hailey's cherished companion. As soon as she could walk, Hailey dragged that bear everywhere she went. Now four years old, she still clings to her favorite bear, and Teddy goes along whenever Hailey spends the night at Bop and GaGa's house.

One morning during a visit from Hailey, I picked up Teddy and pretended to talk for him. Disguising my voice I growled, "Wake up, Hailey.

It's time for breakfast." Still half asleep, Hailey rolled over and giggled, "Oh, GaGa, teddy bears don't talk. They're just for hugging."

"That's true," I answered. "And everyone needs a teddy to hug."

—Susan

Almost every little girl and boy has a favorite teddy bear. Watch the excitement on your child's face when you announce, "Let's have a Teddy Bear Picnic!" It's easy, it's fun, and everyone—young and old alike—will have a beary good time!

Don't forget to ask each of your guests to bring a favorite bear. Then gather everyone together in the backyard or at a park. Spread out a traditional red and white picnic cloth or make your own out of teddy-bear fabric.

ACTIVITIES

 Sit in a circle and ask the children to introduce their bear by name and share something special about it.

 Award prizes for the oldest, the best dressed, the funniest looking, and the fanciest bear. Have enough categories so that every bear wins a prize. Award teddy-bear stickers for the children and doll hats for the bears.

- Fill a small jar with gummi bears and ask each child to guess how many bears are in the jar. For very young children use teddy grahams and limit the number to ten. The winner gets to keep the jar of goodies.

- Before guests arrive hide a jar of honey, bananas, boxes of teddy grahams, and stuffed animals in the "forest." Invite the children to find these items on a scavenger hunt. Award small prizes to everyone.

- Purchase a bear mask or make one from a paper plate and piece of elastic. Play hide-and-seek. Children wear the bear mask when it's their turn to "seek."

- Play "The Teddy Bears' Picnic" song and have the children dance to the music with their teddy bears.

PACK A BASKET OF TEDDY BEAR TREATS

Using bear-shaped cookie cutters, cut bread into bear shapes for the sandwiches. Spread bread with "bear food"—peanut butter mixed with honey and topped with sliced bananas. Or provide circles of bread covered with peanut butter and have children use raisins to make a bear face. Yum!

At this picnic no ants are allowed—except for crunchy "ants on a log." Stuff celery with cream cheese or peanut butter and dot with raisins.

Bake your favorite cupcakes, frost with chocolate frosting, and decorate with gummi or graham bears. Or create "furry" frosting by stirring in shredded coconut or adding chocolate sprinkles on top.

Nothing quenches a little cub's thirst like Bear Milk. Just add a dash of cinnamon and a squirt of honey to a glass of cold milk.

TIME TO SAY GOOD-BYE

Arrange the children in a circle and read *The Teddy Bears' Picnic* or a Winnie the Pooh story. As you wave good-bye, remind everyone—teddy bears and people—that when they get home, it's time to cuddle up in their "caves" and hibernate for a short afternoon nap. 🐾

All things bright and beautiful,
All creatures great and small,
All things wise and wonderful:
The Lord God made them all.

CECIL F. ALEXANDER

Good-bye, Mrs. Snail

SHIRLEY DOBSON

Our now-grown daughter, Danae, loved every aspect of childhood and was reluctant to leave it. As a small child, she would place her dolls on a shelf and role-play with her teddy bears, stuffed rabbits, and kittens. Each one had a special name and would take its turn sleeping with her.

I earned my own special name during that time. I had decided to give Danae and her friends a tea party. We set out the good china, cookies, and napkins. Then Danae helped me create pretend names for all her friends. We had Mrs. Perry, Mrs. White, and Mrs. Green, and I was Mrs. Snail (I didn't ask any questions!). The names stuck, and every time we put on a tea party after that morning, I was Mrs. Snail.

I thoroughly enjoyed being "Mom" in those days and wished they could have gone on forever. And I think Danae felt the same way. Her stuffed animals, old phonograph records, and other toys were cherished possessions throughout her grade-school years.

Enjoy the golden moments of dolls and teddy bears, because all too soon the magical years of pretending are left behind.

But kids do grow up. When Danae turned thirteen, her interests began to change. The stuffed animals went untouched in their various homes, and the familiar records began collecting dust. About a year later, Danae went through her toys and possessions, stacking them neatly and leaving them in front of [her younger brother] Ryan's bedroom door. I discovered them there with a note that brought tears to my eyes. It read:

Dear Ryan,
These are yours now.
Take good care of them like I have.
Love, Danae

That brief message made me realize that Danae had left childhood behind. She was now a young woman entering an exciting new phase of learning and maturing. And as she changed, I needed to change my approach to her as a parent.

In God's holy wisdom, such transitions are part of His plan for each of us. Nothing remains the same. The Lord presents us with new challenges and opportunities in every stage of this life. That's not a bad thing! When we acknowledge that God is in control of our lives and our families, it becomes easier for us to embrace change. ✦

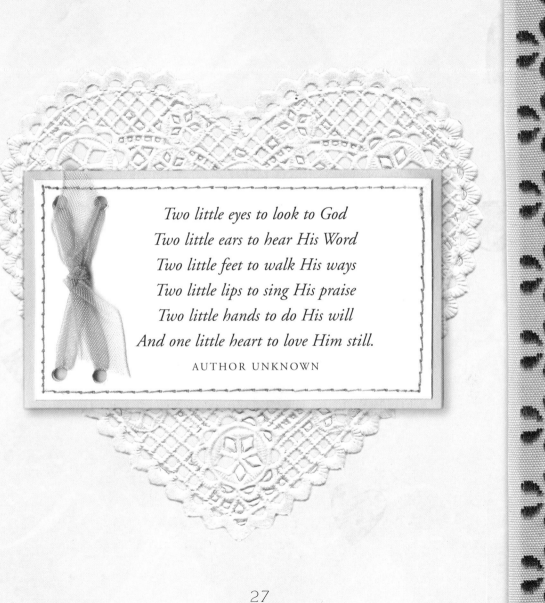

Two little eyes to look to God
Two little ears to hear His Word
Two little feet to walk His ways
Two little lips to sing His praise
Two little hands to do His will
And one little heart to love Him still.

AUTHOR UNKNOWN

Cozy Bedtime Rituals

★ ★ ★

Too often the simple pleasure of a bedtime ritual can be pushed aside in our stressful, too-much-to-do world. But when a mother takes just a few unhurried minutes each evening to establish a loving nighttime routine, it can become the most golden moment of the day for her as well as for her child.

★ Every night when you kneel by the bed to pray with your children, ask them if they want to pray about something special. Be sure to include their requests as you pray together.

★ When you tuck your children into bed, ask each one of them, "Who does Mommy love?" Teach your children to touch their cheeks and reply, "Me!"

★ When children are younger, let them choose a book for you to read. When they are older, occasionally ask them to read to you.

★ Turn down the sheets and fluff the pillows every night. Sometimes, leave a little gift on the pillow—a poem, a paper heart that says "I love you," a page of stickers, a pretty hair ribbon, a Matchbox® car—something that tells your children that you think they're special.

★ On dark, stormy nights, anticipate your children's fears. Make a pallet of blankets on your bedroom floor and invite them to bring their pillows and sleep in your bedroom.

★ If you have a cherished childhood teddy or dolly, let your child sleep with it on specials occasions or when he or she is feeling sad.

★ As your children step out of their baths on chilly nights, wrap each of them in a warm, soft towel that you've pulled straight from the dryer.

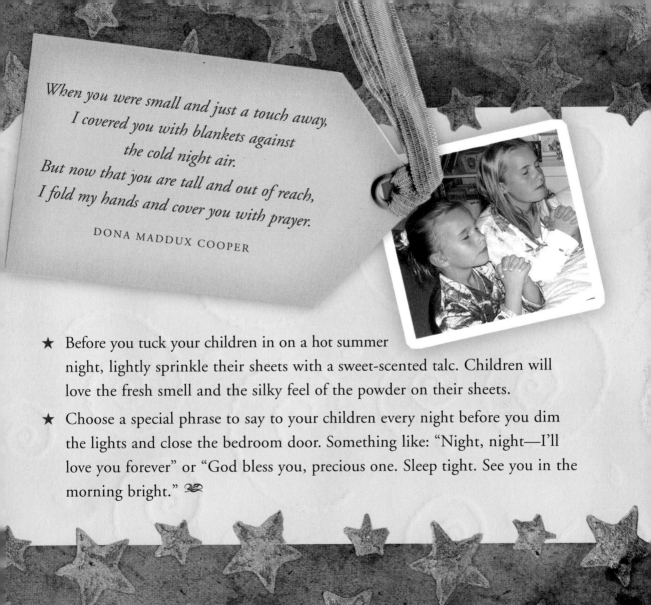

> When you were small and just a touch away,
> I covered you with blankets against
> the cold night air.
> But now that you are tall and out of reach,
> I fold my hands and cover you with prayer.
>
> DONA MADDUX COOPER

★ Before you tuck your children in on a hot summer night, lightly sprinkle their sheets with a sweet-scented talc. Children will love the fresh smell and the silky feel of the powder on their sheets.

★ Choose a special phrase to say to your children every night before you dim the lights and close the bedroom door. Something like: "Night, night—I'll love you forever" or "God bless you, precious one. Sleep tight. See you in the morning bright." ✍

KEEPSAKE Memories

Here are some wonderful ways to celebrate the birth of your baby—or to commemorate any birthday or special occasion. Not only will your children love these ideas, you will be creating cherished memories.

- ❦ Write a letter to your children on each of their birthdays. In these letters tell them how much you love them, describe their best attributes, and mention some of the special events in the past year of their lives. Store the letters in a keepsake box, journal, or scrapbook to present to each child on his or her eighteenth birthday.

- ❦ Plant a tree to commemorate your child's birth. Then, on each birthday, take a picture of your child standing near the tree. If there's no space to plant a tree, check with your state's forestry department to find out how to donate a tree in your child's honor.

- ❦ Create a special set of keepsakes by buying a newspaper on the day your child is born and on every subsequent birthday.

- ❦ To honor your child's birth, make a donation to a charity for needy or orphaned children. Keep the receipt and some information about the

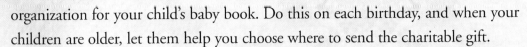

organization for your child's baby book. Do this on each birthday, and when your children are older, let them help you choose where to send the charitable gift.

❧ Every day look through the change in your pocket or purse. Sort out the coins inscribed with the year of your child's birth. Keep the coins in a special piggy bank and count them each birthday. Eventually you will need to open a bank account, but continue the ritual until your child goes off to college or leaves home. ❧

*For all of us,
today's experiences are
tomorrow's memories.*

BARBARA JOHNSON

Springtime Surprises

"Spring is here!" said the bumblebee.
"How do you know?" asked the old oak tree.
"I just saw a daffodil
dancing with a lily on a windy hill."

CHILDREN'S RHYME

Spring!

When you wake up whistling…

When an afternoon rain tastes sweet…

When lilac-scented breezes kiss your face…

When cherry blossoms fall from trees like pink confetti…

It must be spring!

Many mothers say that spring is their favorite time of year. Dew-laden flowers sparkle in the garden, meadowlarks

splash in birdbaths, and on bright sunshiny days children play outside again!

Spring is also the season for planting. Not only is it the time of year for planting a garden, but spring is also an ideal time for sowing seeds of wonder in a child's heart. ❧

I love spring anywhere, but if I could choose I would always greet it in a garden.

RUTH STOUT

Springtime Surprises

❧

Spring is full of sunny surprises. Baby birds peek out of nests, colorful buds decorate tree branches, and crocuses pop up through the once-frozen ground. As God resurrects the wintry world with a glorious spring, it is a perfect time to awaken your children to the wonder of His creation.

Borrow a book about wildflowers from the library. Then take your children on a nature walk and see how many different kinds of flowers

you can find. Trillium appears when the first robins return from their winter homes. Help your children discover the trillium's perfect pattern of threes. Forget-me-nots bloom in late spring, and children love to feel the "mouse ear" leaves.

Gather bits of colored yarn, lint from the clothes dryer, and excelsior, the grass-like nesting from Easter baskets. Put them on a porch railing or the branch of a tree for the birds to use to line their nests.

One of God's greatest surprises in nature is the miraculous transformation of a plain caterpillar into a beautiful butterfly. You might want to adopt a fuzzy little caterpillar and watch the miracle unfold right before your eyes. Do a little research about types of caterpillars online. ✎

Taking Wing

LYNN D. MORRISSEY

It was late spring, and my young daughter, Sheridan, and I were
planning some special mother-daughter activities. With a little trepidation,
I allowed her to "adopt" a caterpillar from a local birdseed store as one way for us
to make a memory together.

Gingerly placing the jar with the striped caterpillar she'd dubbed Sunrise in a
darkened corner of our kitchen, Sheridan promised to feed her, tend her, and keep
her at a respectable distance from me. Though never fond of things that creep,
I was fascinated by the assurance that this tiny insect would soon morph into a big,
beautiful butterfly. I could hardly wait to share this experience with my daughter.

One momentous morning Sunrise crawled to the lid of the jar, tenaciously
attached herself, and shed her skin. In the stillness of magical moments, she
revealed a chrysalis of shimmering green and unseen dreams… and…she waited…

And so did we…

During the ensuing weeks, Sheridan and I shared with each other our hopes for the tiny tenant residing inside the chrysalis. And, in the process, Sheridan began sharing her own hopes and dreams with me.

One day, in the fullness of time, we beheld a brilliant butterfly, her orange-and-black stained-glass wings trembling inside the jar. We, too, trembled at her breathtaking beauty and at the thought of letting her go. Mustering our courage, we took Sunrise to the garden to free her, praying that she'd linger among the lilacs awhile. She circled above the purple petals and then suddenly flew to the treetops. Alighting for just an instant, she fluttered her wings. They were like little rays of sunshine flashing black branches. Then she ascended higher still and finally disappeared from our sight.

Sheridan and I knew that we could never replace Sunrise, but we decided to adopt a caterpillar every spring and raise it together. And I promised God that I would nurture my own little "butterfly" whose childhood was flitting away with great speed—and that one day I would love her enough to let her take wing, just as we had done for Sunrise. 🦋

Gardening Together

Invite your children to garden with you. Perhaps they can plant fast-growing sunflower seeds or little strawberry plants that will yield lush fruit in a few months. If you plant snapdragons, children will love playing with the puppet-like blossoms—just as you did when you were young.

Whenever you're in the garden with your child—whether you're planting seeds, pulling weeds, or watering flowers—talk about how faith grows. To flourish spiritually, we need to plant seeds of faith by reading God's Word, pull the weeds of negative behaviors, and water our soul with prayer and praise.

The kiss of sun for pardon,
The song of the birds for mirth,
One is nearer God's heart in a garden
Than anywhere else on earth.
DOROTHY FRANCES GURNEY

FIVE ROWS
OF "LETTUCE"

Let us be faithful.
Let us be unselfish.
Let us be loyal.
Let us love one another.
Let us be truthful.
AUTHOR UNKNOWN

Little princess, full of grace,
Dressed in satin, pearls, and lace....

A Princess Tea Party

❧

What little girls—and some big girls, too—haven't dreamed of being a princess?

You'll hear squeals of delight and see radiant smiles when your young guests arrive for a springtime princess tea. Invite each little miss to don her favorite princess dress for this royal affair.

THE ROYAL CASTLE

Set a tea table with a tablecloth and cover it with white or pink tulle. Make sugar cookies using crown- or heart-shaped cookie cutters, and decorate with pink or white frosting and sprinkles. A toy castle or a castle cake (you can order one from a bakery!) would be a perfect centerpiece. Scatter pink rose petals or pink confetti around the castle. Transform chairs into thrones by wrapping them in tulle and tying it at the back with a satin bow. Let each bow's streamers flow!

A BEAUTIFUL REFLECTION

Before the festivities begin, invite the princesses to apply lip gloss, a touch of blush, and scented hand lotion. When the young royals are finished applying their makeup and lotion, it's time for their jewelry and crowns.

Her Majesty's Jewelry

Purchase supplies from craft stores so each guest can make her own princess necklace and bracelet.

Her Majesty's Crown

Cut silk or live flowers, leaving a two-inch stem on each. Arrange them in a circle, weave them together, and twist with florist wire. Tie colorful ribbon streamers at the back of the flower crowns.

Qualities of God's Little Princesses

After all the girls are jeweled and crowned, explain that as daughters of the Heavenly King, it is much more important to be pretty on the inside than it is on the outside. Then read about the following lovely attributes from the Bible.

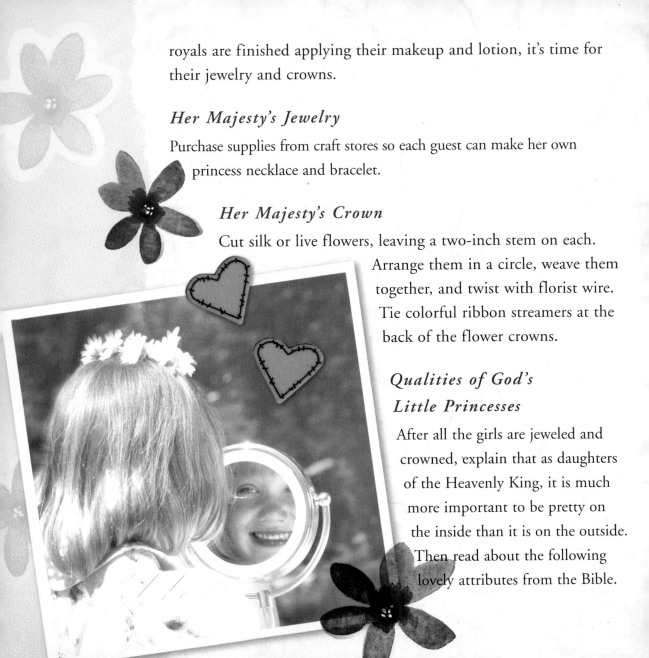

Love Joy Peace Patience Kindness
Goodness Faithfulness Gentleness Self-control

GALATIANS 5:22–23

For party favors write the above words on parchment or other pretty paper, roll up, and tie with a pink ribbon. Let the guests know that they will each receive their very own copy to take home.

HAPPILY EVER AFTER

When it's time for the princesses to return to their castles, present each guest with her own parchment scroll. Wish them God's blessings for many "happily ever after" days.

TEATIME BLESSING

Lord, grant that our time together be steeped in serenity, sweetened by sharing, and surrounded by the warm fragrance of your love.

47

A Teatime Tradition

Each year Emilie Barnes has a tea party to celebrate her granddaughter's birthday. One year Mrs. Barnes searched antique gift shops until she found enough dainty demitasse teacups for each young guest to have one of her own. She let each girl pick out a cup, and then she explained that all the teacups were beautiful—just as every single one of the girls was beautiful. Then she asked them to look closely at the demitasse teacups. Each cup had tiny cracks or chips. She told the girls that, as they grew older, things might happen in their lives that would cause them to feel disappointed or hurt. Mrs. Barnes said that such chips and cracks come into everyone's life, but to always remember that, just as the teacups were still beautiful, the girls would be, too.

I love things that bear the touch of time,
chips and all—they're more beautiful than perfection.

VICTORIA MAGAZINE

Easter Story Cookies

Of course Easter is the most important springtime day of all. And baking these "sleeping cookies"—on the evening before Easter Sunday—is a wonderful way to teach your children about the crucifixion and resurrection of Jesus Christ.

1 cup whole pecans

Ziploc® quart bag

Wooden spoon

1 teaspoon vinegar

3 egg whites

Pinch of salt

1 cup sugar

6-ounce package chocolate chips

Tape

Bible

🌱 Preheat oven to 300 degrees.

- Place pecans in Ziploc® bag and let the children beat them with a wooden spoon to break them into small pieces. Explain that after Jesus was arrested, He was beaten by the Roman soldiers. Read John 19:1–3.

- Pour vinegar on a sponge. Then pass the sponge around and let the children smell the vinegar. Pour 1 teaspoon of vinegar into a mixing bowl. Explain that when Jesus was thirsty on the cross, He was given vinegar to drink. Read John 19:28–30.

- Add egg whites to the vinegar. Eggs represent life. Explain that Jesus died so we can live forever. Read John 10:10–11.

🐾 Sprinkle a little salt into each child's hands. Let them taste it and then put a pinch of salt into the bowl. Explain that the salt represents the salty tears shed by Jesus' followers. Read Luke 23:27.

🐾 Add 1 cup of sugar. Explain that the sweetest part of the story is that Jesus died because He loves us. Read John 3:16.

🐾 Beat with a mixer on high speed for 12 to 15 minutes until stiff peaks form. Explain that the color white represents the purity of Jesus. Fold in the broken nuts and chocolate chips. As the white mixture covers the nuts and chips, explain that if we believe in Jesus, He will forgive and cover over our sins and make us white as snow. Read Isaiah 1:18.

🐾 Drop the mixture by teaspoonfuls onto a wax paper-covered cookie sheet. Explain that each mound represents the rocky tomb where Jesus' body was laid. Read Matthew 27:57–60.

🐾 Place the cookie sheet in the oven, close the door, and turn the oven off. Give each child a piece of tape to symbolically seal the oven door. Explain that Jesus' tomb was sealed. Read Matthew 27:65–66.

🥚 Go to bed! Explain to the children that they may feel sad to leave the cookies in the oven—and that Jesus' followers felt very sad when they left Jesus lying in the tomb. Read John 16:20, 22.

🥚 On Easter morning gather the children around and unseal the oven. Give everyone a cookie. As the children take a bite, make sure they notice that the cookies are hollow. They'll be amazed just as, on that first Easter Day, Jesus' followers were amazed to find the tomb open and empty. Read Matthew 28:1–6.

He is not here;
for He is risen!

MATTHEW 28:6

53

The Blessings of Prayer

❧

The most precious gift a mother can give her children is to guide them toward faith in Jesus Christ. Praying with them and teaching them how to pray will not only help build their faith; it will also bless them for a lifetime.

Each morning before your children leave home or start their day, hold hands and pray with them. Ask for God's guidance, protection, and peace in their lives.

Teach your children to thank the Lord for their food at every meal. In the evening have every family member add a sentence thanking God for the best part of their day.

Kneel with your children at bedtime and ask God to bless and protect them through the night. Thank Him for one special quality in each child. Also encourage your children to share any worries or hurts from the day and together place those concerns in the Lord's loving hands.

Select specific Scripture verses to pray for your children. To personalize God's truth for them, replace the word "you" with each of their names. ❧

The LORD bless you and keep you;
the LORD make his face shine upon you
and be gracious to you;
the LORD turn his face toward you
and give you peace.

NUMBERS 6:24-26, NIV

KEEPSAKE Memories

One of the dearest sounds children can hear is the voice of their mother praying for them. Imagine what these prayer mementos below, as well as the knowledge of their mother's faithful prayers throughout their lives, will mean to them as an adult.

- Cut out a paper heart, write your child's name on it, and tuck it in your Bible. On the back of the heart, write a special prayer and verse—one you've chosen specifically for your child.

- Keep a separate prayer journal for each of your children. On the first page of their journal, trace their handprint and let them decorate the page. Explain that you will place your own hand on top of their handprint when you pray for them.

- At the beginning of each year, make matching bookmarks for you and your children. Include a special Bible verse that you will use throughout the year when you pray for each of them.

Think of prayer as little bricks
to lay on the pathway to eternity.

JANE JARRELL

Summertime Fun

It was a lovely day of blue skies and gentle breezes.
Bees buzzed, birds tootled, and squirrels bustled to and fro,
getting their suntan in the bright sunshine.
In a word, all Nature smiled.

P.G. WODEHOUSE

Summer!

Watching lightning bugs dance…

    Building sandcastles at the seashore…

        Pitching a tent under a star-studded sky…

            Lingering on the porch with the scent of lilacs in the air…

Ah, those lazy, barefoot summer days—something about them just makes our hearts smile.

While out on a summer hike, a family discovered an abandoned tree house near the edge of the campground where they were staying. They christened the little house "The Happy Place" because they could easily imagine all the fun and adventure the children once had there.

Those three words—*the happy place*—speak of what mothers hope their children's summer days will be. Good times, carefree adventures, and happy places of the heart. ✑

Memory is a child walking along a seashore.
You never can tell what small pebble he will pick up
and store away among his treasured things.

PIERCE HARRIS

Summer Fun

At the beginning of summer, the days seem to stretch before us like a lazy cat waking up from a nap on a sunny windowsill. But before we know it, there's crispness in the morning hours and pumpkins are budding on the vine. Here are some ideas that are a perfect fit for the slower, mellow days of sunshine.

Watch children's faces light up when you tell them they can make their very own ice cream. It's simple, fun, and delicious!

1 small coffee can with lid	1 tablespoon sugar
1 large coffee can with lid	Ice cubes as needed
1 cup heavy cream	3 tablespoons rock salt
1 teaspoon vanilla extract	

Combine cream, vanilla, and sugar in small coffee can. Secure cover on can. Place the smaller can inside the larger can.   In the gap between the two cans, pack ice and rock salt. Secure the lid on the larger can. Roll the can on the floor

for 20 minutes. Remove lids. If mixture has hardened, serve. If not, continue rolling until ice cream is thick enough to serve.

🐚 Whether your family is camping in the wild or sleeping in a backyard tent, they'll have fun making hobo popcorn. Cut an 18-inch square of heavy-duty aluminum foil for each serving. Place 1 teaspoon of cooking oil and 1 tablespoon of popcorn in the center of each square. Gather up the corners of the foil to make a pouch that looks like a hobo's knapsack. Seal the edges well. Using heavy string, tie the corners of the pouch to a long-handled roasting stick. Place the pouch directly on hot coals and shake often until all the corn is popped. Carefully open and season the popcorn with melted butter and salt.

🐚 A watermelon feed is great fun on a sweltering summer day. Choose a place where you and the kids can let the juice dribble down your chins. Have a contest to see who can spit the seeds the longest distance! ✐

*In this heartwarming story, Pastor Max Lucado shares
a tender message that goes far beyond the summertime wonder
of children and lemonade stands.*

The Lemonade Stand

MAX LUCADO

"Lemonade, 5¢."

The *e* is larger than the *L*. The *m* is uppercased; all the other letters are lowered. The last two letters, *de,* curve downward because the artist ran out of room on the poster.

Norman Rockwell would have loved it.

Two girls sit on the sidewalk in little chairs behind a little table. The six-year-old is the cashier. She monitors a plastic bowl of change. The four-year-old is the waitress. She handles the ice. Pours the drinks. Stacks and restacks the paper cups.

Behind them, seated on the grass, is Dad. He leans against an oak tree and smiles as he witnesses his daughters' inauguration into capitalism.

Business has been steady. The Saturday-afternoon stream of patrons has nearly emptied the pitcher. The bottom of the cashier's bowl is covered with thirty-five cents of change. With the exception of a few spills, the service has been exceptional. No complaints. Many compliments.

Part of the success, though, has been due to the marketing strategy. Our street doesn't get much traffic, so we did a little advertising. As my daughters painted the sign, I called several families in the neighborhood and invited them to the grand opening of our lemonade stand. So all of our clients, thus far, had been partial.

I was proud of myself. I leaned back against the tree. Closed my eyes. Turned up the radio I had brought. And listened to the baseball game.

Then I heard an unfamiliar voice.

"I'll have a cup of lemonade, please."

I opened my eyes. It was a customer. A real customer. An unsolicited neighbor who had driven by, seen the sign, stopped, and ordered a drink.

Uh-oh, I thought. Our service was about to be tested.

Andrea, the four-year-old, grabbed a cup that had already been used.

"Get a clean cup," I whispered.

"Oh," she giggled, and got a clean cup.

She opened the ice bucket, looked in, and then

looked back at me. "Daddy, we are out of ice."

The patron overheard her. "That's OK. I'll take it warm."

She picked up the pitcher and poured. Syrupy sugar oozed out of the pitcher. "Daddy, there's just a little bit."

Our customer spoke again. "That's fine. I don't want much."

"I hope you like it sweet," I said under my breath.

She handed the cup to the man, and he handed her a dollar.

She gave it to Jenna.

Jenna turned to me. "Daddy, what do I do?" (We weren't used to such big bills.)

I stuck my hands in my pockets; they were empty.

"Uh, we don't have any…" I began.

Whatever is true, whatever is noble, whatever is right, whatever is pure, whatever is lovely, whatever is admirable— if anything is excellent or praiseworthy— think about such things.

PHILIPPIANS 4:8, NIV

"No problem," he said, smiling. "Just keep the change."

I smiled sheepishly. He thanked the girls. Told them they were doing a great job. Climbed back into his car. And drove off.

Quite a transaction, I thought. *We give him a warm, partially filled cup of lemonade syrup, and he gives us a compliment and a payment twenty times too much.*

I had set out to teach the girls about free enterprise.

They ended up with a lesson on grace.

And so had I. For all the theologizing we preachers do about God's grace, the kind stranger modeled it better than the best of sermons state it. ✍

Each day comes bearing its own gifts.
Untie the ribbons.

RUTH ANN SCHUBACKER

68

Sunflower Delight

Help your child create this fun and simple flower to place in a vase for a sweet table centerpiece or to give as a surprise gift for the grandparents.

1 plain white paper plate   Paper-towel tube $^1/2$ cup sunflower seeds

Construction paper 8 $^1/2$ x 11 (1 green and 3-6 yellow)

Make the stem of the sunflower by wrapping the piece of green construction paper around the paper-towel tube; secure it with glue or tape. Trace your child's handprints on yellow construction paper. Cut out six to eight handprints depending on the size of their hand. Glue or staple the handprints all around the edge of the paper plate. Spread glue in the middle of the flower. Sprinkle sunflower seeds onto the glue, press, and let dry. Flatten the top of the stem and staple it to the special sunflower. 🌿

KEEPSAKE
Memories

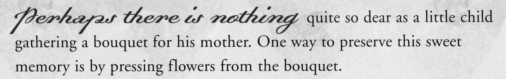

Perhaps there is nothing quite so dear as a little child gathering a bouquet for his mother. One way to preserve this sweet memory is by pressing flowers from the bouquet.

- ❧ Remove the flowers' stems. Then lay the flowers flat on a sheet of tissue paper and cover with a second sheet. Place between the pages of a heavy book and leave undisturbed for two or three weeks.

- ❧ Carefully remove the flowers and place them in a pattern you like on the front of blank cards or onto stiff artists' paper available at craft stores.

- ❧ The pressed flowers will be fragile, so lift them with a pair of tweezers. Then, using a toothpick dipped in white glue, apply a small amount of glue to the back of the flower.

- ❧ For extra protection, cover the paper and flowers with clear, self-adhesive contact paper.

70

A rose can say I love you.
Orchids can enthrall.
But a weed bouquet in a chubby fist—
Oh my, that says it all!

ANONYMOUS

I have no greater joy
than to hear that my children
are walking in the truth.

3 JOHN 1:4, NIV

71

Autumn Gatherings

Winter is an etching,
spring a watercolor,
summer an oil painting,
and autumn a mosaic of them all.

STANLEY HOROWITZ

Autumn!

The sun rises later each morning, and autumn leaves crochet together to form red and yellow archways before they fall silently on the garden path. Autumn is a gentle season—a season for *gathering* and a season for *remembering*.

- It seems like just yesterday when you cradled your newborn baby in your arms, and now you are gathering school supplies for her first day of school. May this be a gentle reminder to cherish the days of childhood because, like the seasons, these precious days pass so quickly.

- Last week warm sunshine kissed suntanned cheeks. Today rain clouds gather in the distance, but tagging along with the clouds is a brilliant rainbow. Enjoy this gentle reminder of God's promises and of His faithfulness to keep those promises.

- Somehow it doesn't seem possible that a year has passed since the last annual Thanksgiving homecoming. Aunts, uncles, cousins, and grandparents all gather around a bountiful table, hold hands, and bow grateful hearts in thankful praise. Celebrate this gentle reminder of God's continued blessings.

Autumn is a time of harvest,
of gathering together.

EDWIN WAY TEAL

The First Day of School

Nothing tugs at a mother's heartstrings quite as much as that day when her child, all dressed up and carrying a colorful new lunchpail, heads off to the first day of school. You can keep a memory of this historic event in a number of special ways.

- Take a photograph of your child on the first day of school. Then, on each subsequent first day of school until your child graduates, take a photo at the same location if possible. Record your child's height on the back of the photo or on the wall that served as a backdrop. What fun to track how much your child grows and see how fashions and hairstyles change over the years.

- Have a special treat ready when your child returns home from that first day. Sit together and leisurely talk about how the day went. Encourage your child to share about new friends, the day's activities, and first impressions of the teacher. Record some of your child's thoughts and keep them with the first-day-of-school picture.

- In a journal or on a sheet of paper, pen your thoughts about this milestone day. Write a special prayer for your children as they step outside the nest.

Mothers hold their
children's hands for a while...
their hearts, forever.

AUTHOR UNKNOWN

Keep This for Me

Most mothers collect and cherish their children's artwork. The refrigerator is the first place to display a budding artist's creations. But before long popsicle-stick sculptures, seed mosaics, and clay paperweights fill every nook and cranny of the house. If you long for extra room to store and display your children's art, consider these ideas.

- Hang clotheslines in your children's bedrooms and attach their artwork with colored clothespins.

- Instead of using a wallpaper border in the children's rooms, make a border with their artwork.

- Attach a scenic drawing to the back of an aquarium or fishbowl.

- Scan your children's artwork. Be sure to include the date, a description of where it was created, and what inspired it. Save the art on a computer disk or create a family Web site for displaying your children's masterpieces.

- Mothers without scanners can photograph the art, reproduce it on color copiers, laminate or protect it with acid-free covers, and save it in a three-ring binder.

- Smaller pieces of art can be digitally copied onto mugs, playing cards, mouse pads, personal gift cards, or stationary.

For centuries handmade quilts have been among a family's most treasured heirlooms. Today twenty-first-century mothers scan their children's artwork and mementos onto the computer, design quilt squares, and sew them together to give as precious birthday, graduation, or wedding gifts.

You never realize how much your mother loves you till you explore the attic and find every letter you ever sent her, every finger painting, clay pot, bead necklace, Easter chicken, cardboard Santa Claus, paper lace Mother's Day card, and school report since day one.

PAM BROWN

Umbrellas & Stars

There is something almost magical about the smell of dusty roads after the first rainfall of autumn. Perhaps it's the mischievous combination of first rains, cool crisp mornings, and warm Indian-summer nights that beckons us to play just a little longer before the frosty days of winter arrive.

- Organize an umbrella parade. It doesn't have to be raining! Children dress up in boots and slickers and pop open their most colorful umbrellas and march around the neighborhood. Find someone who can beat a drum or herald some notes on a bugle. If there are no musicians, use a boom box with John Philip Sousa marching music. After the parade, children will enjoy a treasure hunt where the goal is to find as many objects as they can to represent each color in the rainbow: red, orange, yellow, green, blue, and purple. End the umbrella day by serving Rainbow Sugar Cookies. Divide white frosting (canned or homemade) into separate bowls. Add various food colorings to desired intensity before frosting cookies.

- In our fast-paced world, spending time stargazing is almost an indescribable pleasure—for both adults and children. After an early dinner, fill a thermos with hot chocolate and bundle up the family for a stargazing adventure in

the backyard. Snuggle into warm blankets or sleeping bags and watch as the evening sky changes to a velvet backdrop with thousands of sparkling stars. Astronomers say that when the sky is clear, the naked eye can see over five thousand stars in the Milky Way. Books about stargazing are available at the library and the Internet has galaxy maps and information about dates and times of special celestial events. Finding the North Star, Milky Way, and Big Dipper will open your child's heart to a whole galaxy of adventure.

The heavens declare the glory of God; And the firmament shows His handiwork.

PSALM 19:1

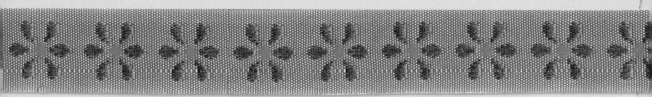

Even before she learned to walk, I took our granddaughter,
little Summer Malu, on her first carousel ride. From that time on,
we shared a love of "round and rounds" with their enchanted horses and
old-fashioned calliope music. When I read the following carousel story,
it was like having happy confetti sprinkled on my heart.
Alice

Carousel Memories

SUSAN FARR-FAHNCKE

It was our first oceanside vacation together, and I had carefully planned all the memory-making fun we would need for the week. We scheduled daily time at the beach, picnics, visits to the aquarium, and other touristy activities. We had a room with the view, sand in our toes, and all the breathtaking sunsets a family could want. And rain.

When the first rain hit our sleepy little beach, we moved our vacation activities three blocks over to the "town" part of Seaside. We soon discovered a little indoor carousel smack-dab in the center of the mall. The traditional happy carousel song coming from the old-fashioned merry-go-round beckoned my delighted children. I grinned at this unexpected find and laughed out loud as I watched my children sparkle with each go 'round. They asked for more, more, more rides until the carousel closed for the day. After that wonderful afternoon, whenever the rain hit, there were no complaints at all! My children happily piled into the car for their new, all-time favorite activity—riding the carousel.

I also realized that, during all our expensive vacations, boardwalk visits, and even trips to Disneyland (the Happiest Place on Earth), I had never seen such pure delight on their little faces as I did when they were on that merry-go-round. With our rapidly filling "stamp" card in hand, Noah and Maya became favorites at the mall. Even the kind lady, who stamped their cards, sensed that special memories were in the making and often gave free rides.

These fun-filled days passed by quickly, and when the last day of our vacation arrived, we were sad to leave our sleepy little beach town. But the time had come.

With our bags packed and loaded into the car, we waved good-bye and headed toward home.

I suddenly made a sharp right turn, and moments later I drove the car into the mall's parking lot. My children's unhappy faces quickly broke into delighted grins as I told them, "One more time!" I watched with a catch in my heart as they enjoyed a final ride on the old carousel, and I realized that true bliss isn't planned, it isn't purchased (at least in this case it didn't cost much more than a dollar), and it isn't necessarily what we picture when we set off to make memories. I kept my kids' carousel stamp card, and when I look at it, I remember the joy found amid the rainstorms and the sound of my children's laughter as they rode on an old carousel.

*You don't really understand human nature
unless you know why a child on a
merry-go-round will wave at his parents
every time around—and why
his parents will always wave back.*

WILLIAM D. TAMMEUS

A Fireman's Red-Hot Party

Only you can prevent forest fires.

SMOKEY THE BEAR

Flashing lights! Shiny red fire trucks! Ladders that reach into the sky! Cute Dalmatian puppies! Everything about a firefighter's party will appeal to the younger set. The brave men and women, who not only put out fires but

also save others from peril—including the family cat that ventured too far out on a limb—can spark a little one's dreams. At one time or another in a little boy's life, he dreams of becoming a fireman, and some little girls do, too. So a firefighter's party is guaranteed to be a red-hot hit!

To make the party a truly unforgettable experience, arrange a tour of your local fire station. It's free!

At some fire stations the firemen will demonstrate how they slide down the pole and use the water hose. The children are often invited to take turns sitting in a fire truck with a fireman. He may allow them to switch on the red flashing lights and activate the siren for a few seconds. If the station has a Dalmation, the children can pet the dog, too.

After an exciting tour of the firehouse, go to a local park or back to your home. Decorate in red—red cups, red plates, and white napkins with Dalmatian-black spots.

Set up a firefighters' obstacle course in your backyard so guests can hurry down a slide, douse a pretend fire with a garden hose, and save a stuffed animal stuck in a tree with a clothespin.

For lunch, serve hot dogs with all the trimmings and one of these two "firehouse" desserts.

CHARRED BANANAS

1 12-inch square of heavy-duty aluminum foil

1 whole banana cut in half lengthwise

$^1/_4$ cup chocolate chips

$^1/_4$ cup miniature marshmallows

Sprinkle chocolate chips and miniature marshmallows onto bananas; wrap in foil and secure. Cook on the barbecue for ten minutes.

DALMATIAN CAKE

Bake a round cake or cupcakes and frost with white icing. Dot the cake with chocolate icing and chocolate chips to look like the spots on a Dalmatian.

TIME TO SAY "THANK YOU"

After lunch, have the kids draw scenes from their fire station tour and help them write the firemen a thank-you note. Provide extra cupcakes with white frosting for the kids to decorate with chocolate chips and deliver the cupcakes to the fire station along with the children's thank-you notes.

My hero is a fireman because he puts out fires and saves people.

JACOB — AGE 5

Fall Decorating Ideas

Whatever the style of your home décor, God's warm autumn ambience invites you to gather a few cozy splashes of gold, orange, and red and bring them inside.

- Ask your children to select apples, miniature pumpkins, or colorful gourds to use as charming holders for votive candles. Then have an adult cut a candle-sized hole in the top of the item and let the children place the candle inside.

- Kids will enjoy making creative designs by decorating oranges with whole cloves. These simple decorations are fragrant and look attractive in a glass or ceramic bowl.

- Children will love helping with this easy-to-make centerpiece. Cut a hole and place a jelly jar in the center of a small pumpkin. Fill the jar with some water and a variety of seasonal fall wildflowers or yellow chrysanthemums. For a larger centerpiece, use a Mason jar and a bigger pumpkin.

- Choose several ears of Indian corn in varied colors and tie them together with raffia for a festive front-door decoration.

Ask your children to gather leaves of various fall colors to make some fall place-mats. Arrange the leaves between two place-mat-sized sheets of waxed paper. Run a hot iron over the waxed paper to seal the leaves. Cut edges with pinking shears.

Scoop out a soup-bowl-sized pumpkin for each family member. Serve your family's favorite soup in the pumpkin bowls.

The little things we do at home, like putting wildflowers in a vase, are invisible medicine for all the bumps and bruises of family life.

INGRID TROBISCH

KEEPSAKE *Memories*

Thanksgiving, when all the relatives are together, is a perfect time to gather recipes for a keepsake family cookbook. Imagine being able to give your grown children a beautiful book of recipes, household tips, and photographs of family gatherings as a "taste" of their heritage. What a keepsake treasure for generations to come!

- Ask grandparents, aunts, and uncles to contribute their favorite recipes.
- Gather pictures of Dad at the grill, Grandpa carving a turkey, Mom taking pies from the oven, little Suzie stirring up her first batch of cookies, and summertime fun at family picnics.
- Add brief stories of family history and helpful household tips.
- Use a recipe scrapbook kit from a scrapbooking store or simply slide recipes into vinyl sheet protectors and put them in a three-ring binder. Scan the pages so you can print multiple copies.

Oh, give thanks to the LORD,
for He is good!
For His mercy endures forever.

PSALM 136:1

Winter
Wonderland

Snowflakes are
kisses from heaven.

AUTHOR UNKNOWN

The first fall of snow is not only an event,
it is a magical event.
You go to bed in one kind of a world and
wake up in another quite different,
and if this is not enchantment then
where is it to be found?

J. B. PRIESTLEY

Winter!

While rosy-cheeked children snuggle deep in the warm comfort of their beds, the light from a full moon transforms the first dusting of snow into silver frosting.

❧ Smoke curls upward from chimney tops as a trillion diamondlike stars dance with the twinkling lights hanging like icicles from porches decorated for Christmas.

❧ A young mother sighs contentedly, pulls her chair closer to the cozy fire, and curls her stockinged feet under her.

❧ This is her time for reflection, her time for savoring treasured family memories from seasons past.

Once again the wonder of winter has spun its magic.

Let It Snow!

Nothing quite compares to the excitement of awakening on a chilly winter morn, looking out a frosty window intricately decorated with ice mosaics, and discovering that the world outside is blanketed with snow. The squeals of your children as they exclaim, "It's snowing!" bring

back precious memories from your own childhood. It's definitely time to bundle up the family and together create a winter wonderland of snowy fun.

* *Personality Snowmen:* Build several snowmen and dress them up to look like family members.

* *Animal Trackers:* Check out a book about animal tracks from the library. Then see how many different tracks you can recreate by using wooden spoons and small gardening tools.

* *Critter Treats:* Spread peanut butter on bagel halves and sprinkle with birdseed. Use colorful yarn to hang these snacks from tree branches. Or string popcorn or mini shredded-wheat cereal to drape over branches.

* *Snow Baseball:* This fun game is best for two players but more can play by dividing a larger group into teams. Pile up two mounds of snow anywhere between eight and fifteen feet apart depending on the ages of the children. On one mound place four empty soup cans; the other mound is for pitching

snowballs. Each side gets twelve pitches per "inning." If playing with a larger group, take turns pitching. A knocked-over can is a base hit, and four knocked-over cans equal a home run.

❋ *Behold! A Snow Angel:* Find an area where the snow is smooth, clean, and powdery. Lie down on your back. To form angel wings, move your arms

Snowmen fall from heaven... unassembled.

AUTHOR UNKNOWN

from your sides to over your head and then back again. To make the bottom part of the angel's robe, move your legs side to side. Then have someone stand at your feet, grab your hands, and pull you up from the snow.

❊ *Rainbow Angels:* Fill several spray bottles with water that you've mixed with a variety of food colorings. Then go outside and make a row of snow angels. Be sure there's enough space for the angels' wings! When the snow angels are finished, spray them with the colored water. Don't forget the camera!

❊ *No Snow?* Let the children play outdoors with shaving cream and pretend that it's snow. Build snowmen or other creations from piles of shaving cream. Or, stay inside and make some edible snowmen. Fasten the marshmallows together with a toothpick, dress snowmen in licorice-strip scarves, add pretzel sticks for arms, use candy corn for the noses, and raisins for button eyes. Yum!

Oh, the Weather Outside Is Frightful!

When the afternoon sun dips low and the weather outside is frightful, invite kids to a campout adventure inside the house!

INDOOR CAMPOUT

When the guests arrive, get them in the camping mood by watching a classic movie such as *The Wilderness Family* or *Robinson Crusoe*. Spread a blanket in front of the fireplace and serve hamburgers with all the trimmings.

After supper, turn down the lights. Give the happy campers flashlights and send them on a search for stuffed wild animals that you hid beforehand. When the campers return from their hunt, let them help set up camp. Cover chairs and tables with blankets or sheets to make an indoor tent. Put pillows and either extra blankets or sleeping bags inside the tent for bedtime. Once the tent is ready, roast marshmallows in the fireplace or treat them to microwave s'mores.

MICROWAVE S'MORES

For each serving:

    2 graham cracker squares

    1 large marshmallow

    4 squares of a milk chocolate bar

Place a graham cracker square on a paper napkin. Top with chocolate, marshmallow, and the second graham cracker square. Microwave on high for about 30–45 seconds. Cool before eating.

NIGHTY-NIGHT

Sing familiar camp songs before your tired campers crawl into the tent for the night. End your sing-along by either singing "Taps" or simply reciting the words as a prayer.

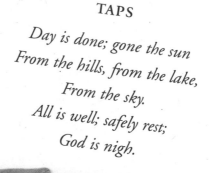

TAPS

Day is done; gone the sun
From the hills, from the lake,
From the sky.
All is well; safely rest;
God is nigh.

Foot Rubs and Giggle Belly

After a glorious day of playing outside, invite your family to warm their feet by a cozy fire. Before putting on cozy socks or slippers, take turns giving each other peppermint foot rubs. Mix one tablespoon peppermint oil into six ounces of unscented lotion. As you gently rub one another's feet, watch the smiles appear.

GIGGLE BELLY GAME

At least four players are needed

The first player lies down on his back. The next player lies down with her head resting on the first player's belly. Continue this pattern until everyone is zigzagged around the floor, each with his or her head on someone else's belly. Close the circle by having the last player put his head on the first player's belly.

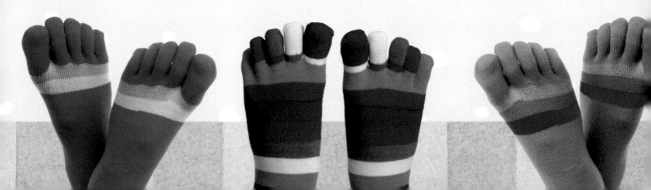

Now that everyone is in position, the first player shouts, "Ha!" The second player responds with a vigorous, "Ha, ha!" The third player takes a turn with "Ha, ha, ha!" Continue around the circle and enjoy all the laughter as heads bounce up and down on bellies. Ha, ha, ha, ha!

A merry heart does good, like medicine...

PROVERBS 17:22

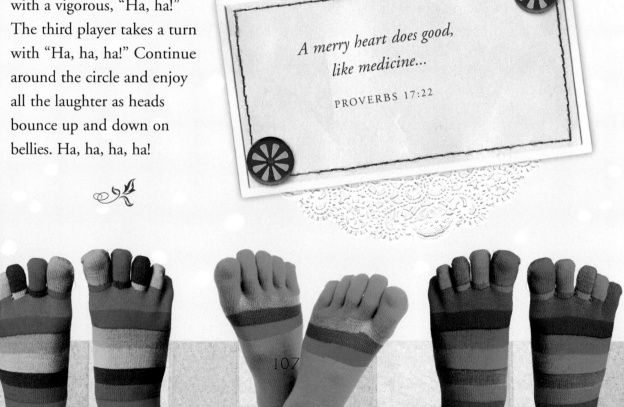

Children love playing dress-up with a trunk full of hats, jewelry, and scarves—but sometimes watching their mothers dress up for a special occasion can be just as delightful.

The Jewelry Box

FAITH ANDREWS BEDFORD

Tonight is our anniversary, and my husband is taking me out. I look through my closet and pick out a deep-green velvet dress with long sleeves and a high neck. It looks wonderful with my mother's seed pearl necklace and my grandmother's tiny pearl earrings.

As I sit at my dressing table, my daughter, Eleanor, perches beside me. She loves to watch me get dressed for special occasions. "Mama," she addresses my reflection in the mirror, "may I pick out your jewelry?"

"Of course," I reply.

She opens the drawer where I keep my jewelry box and begins to sift through the contents. There are the macaroni necklaces she made me in kindergarten and the locket my husband gave me when we were engaged. In a little box Eleanor finds my old Girl Scout pin and some badges.

She holds several pairs of earrings up to her small ears, then discards them. She tries on several necklaces, and shakes her head. At last, with a little cry of delight, she pounces on a pair of long, dangly earrings from Ceylon. They are set with flashing mirrors, obviously left over from the seventies. I wore them with bell-bottoms and tunics. In another box she finds two long ropes of beads from the same era.

She drapes the beads around my neck and hands me the earrings. I put them on and give my head a little shake. The earrings glitter brightly.

"Perfect!" She sighs with pleasure. We grin at each other in the mirror.

As Eleanor twirls out of the room to tell her father that I am almost ready, I remember how, when I was Eleanor's age, I used to watch, entranced, as my own mother prepared for an evening out. While she pinned up her French twist, I would ask her to tell me where each piece had come from.

In a velvet case lay a beautiful garnet necklace and matching earrings. Mother told me that they belonged to her grandmother who wore them to Boston, where she had seen the famous Sarah Bernhardt perform.

The seed pearl necklace had been given to Mother by her godmother as a wedding present. Like me, she always wore it with the tiny pearl earrings her grandmother left her. Now I have inherited both.

My favorite things in the drawer were the gifts my father had given her. In a velvet box was a necklace of rhinestones that glittered with the brilliance of real diamonds. Mother told me they were not diamonds at all, but I thought she still looked like a princess.

The Christmas I was ten, I had saved up enough money to buy Mother some earrings at the five-and-dime: two red plastic bells hung from tiny bows. The edges had been sprinkled with silver glitter. Mother wore them all Christmas Day. She shook her head frequently to show us how they actually made a tinkling sound.

A few days later I came into her room just in time to zip up her black and white taffeta evening dress.

"Will you pick out some earrings for me, dear?" she asked.

Opening her drawer I sorted through the options. *Her dress was pretty*, I thought, *but it needed a bit of color.* I proudly pulled out the little red plastic bells.

"Just the thing," she said, putting them on. I looked at her and thought no one ever was more beautiful.

My husband's voice pulls me back to the present. "Ready?" he asks.

"Almost," I reply, putting Mother's pearls and Grandmother's earrings back into my jewelry box.

As I come down the stairs, my beads swinging and the brass earrings flashing in the light, I look down and see Eleanor's proud face. "You look beautiful," she sighs.

"Only with your help," I reply as I kiss her good night. She will be asleep by the time I return.

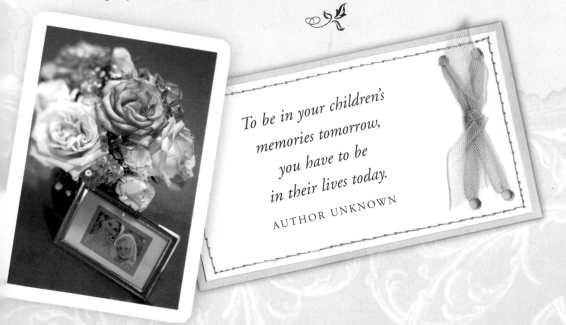

To be in your children's memories tomorrow, you have to be in their lives today.

AUTHOR UNKNOWN

Keeping Christmas

With all that glitters during the holidays, we sometimes forget the timeless message that Christmas was a birthday before it was a holiday. Here's a potpourri of ideas for making simple gifts, creating meaningful memories, and keeping Jesus at the center of your Christmas celebrations.

HEARTS OF LOVE

Use costume jewelry and beads to decorate a box for each of your children. Then, for each child, cut thirty hearts out of construction paper. Write a compliment or a favorite Bible verse on each one and place them in the box you have decorated. Give these keepsake boxes to your children. Be sure to attach a note telling them to read a heart-message each day.

Happy Birthday, Jesus!

Invite your children's friends to a birthday party for Jesus. Decorate as you would for any birthday party. Hang streamers and balloons, provide party hats, and have festive plates and napkins. Ask each guest to bring a gift for a needy child.

Whether you bake a cake or order one from the bakery, have it decorated with the words "Happy birthday, Jesus!" Light candles—a single candle to represent Jesus as the Light of the World or twenty candles representing the centuries since His birth.

Join hands and sing "Happy Birthday" before blowing out the candles.

Even if you don't have a party, you can still have a birthday cake. Before your family opens Christmas presents, light the candles, hold hands, and sing "Happy Birthday" to Jesus.

"Missing You!"

When loved ones can't be with you for the holidays, gather friends and/or family members together a few weeks before Christmas. Hold up a big sign that says, "We Love You!" or "Merry Christmas!" and snap a photo of the gang.

Place the picture in a handsome frame and mail it early enough so it will arrive before Christmas. Also, be sure to have every family member or friend who was photographed sign a card.

Another option is to make a home video. Invite each person you film to both share a special memory and update the recipient on what is happening in his or her life. Close with words of love and a rousing rendition of "We Wish You a Merry Christmas."

Candles of Blessing

After Christmas dessert, place a votive candle at each guest's plate. Begin by lighting the candle of the person on your right and share one quality that makes this person special to you. Continue around the table and ask each guest to light a candle and say something special about the person on his or her right. Although it's a very simple act, there will probably be laughter, tears of joy, and precious memories as candles are lighted and hearts are blessed.

Christmas is the season of love,
a time for gathering together and
celebrating the greatest gift of all—
the arrival of the Savior.

ANONYMOUS

KEEPSAKE Memories

No matter how many heirlooms a mother collects or how many scrapbooks she keeps, no gift from her will ever be more valuable than teaching her children about God's love. That's why giving your son or daughter a bracelet that reminds them of salvation through Jesus Christ is far more than just a gift of jewelry. It's a keepsake treasure that tells the story of the Greatest Gift ever given.

FAITH BRACELETS

Faith bracelets can be purchased at many gift and jewelry stores, but they are also easy to make. Simply select beads that match the colors shown below. For your daughter, use crystal beads, silver spacers, and silver bead wire. For your son, use craft beads and suede or leather cord. Follow basic jewelry-making instructions available at almost all craft stores.

Only God Himself fully appreciates the influence of a Christian mother.

BILLY GRAHAM

The black bead stands for our sin
that separates us from God.

The clear bead stands for
Christ's purity.

The red bead stands for the death
of Jesus on the cross.

The white bead stands for
God's forgiveness.

The green bead stands for
spiritual growth.

The blue bead stands for the
Holy Spirit living in us.

The gold bead stands for
eternity in heaven.

ACKNOWLEDGMENTS

"Goodbye Mrs. Snail" by Shirley Dobson, from *Night Light for Parents* by Dr. James and Shirley Dobson, © 2002 by James Dobson, Inc. Used by permission of Multnomah Publishers, Inc, Sisters, OR.

"Taking Wing" by Lynn D. Morrissey, © 2004. Used by permission of the author. All rights reserved. Original story was printed in *Love Letters to God,* Multnomah Publishers, Sisters OR.

"A Teatime Tradition" based on a story in *Welcome Home* by Emilie Barnes with Anne Christian Buchanan, © 1997, Harvest House Publishers, Eugene, OR.

"Resurrection Cookies" was adapted from a family recipe.

"The Lemonade Stand" by Max Lucado, *In The Eye of the Storm,* © 1991, W Publishing, a division of Thomas Nelson, Inc., Nashville, TN. Used by permission. All rights reserved.

"Carousel Memories" by Susan Farr-Fahncke, © 2005. Used by permission of the author. All rights reserved. Susan Farr-Fahncke is the author of *Angel's Legacy* and contributor to numerous books. She teaches online writing workshops at 2TheHeart.com, email editor@2theheart.com.

"The Jewelry Box" by Faith Andrews Bedford, from *Country Living* magazine. Used by permission of the author. All rights reserved. Faith Andrews Bedford is the author of *Barefoot Summers*, Hearst Books, New York, NY.